The Flightless Years

poems by

Jamie L. Smith

Finishing Line Press
Georgetown, Kentucky

The Flightless Years

Copyright © 2024 by Jamie L. Smith
ISBN 979-8-88838-810-5 First Edition
All rights reserved under International and Pan-American Copyright Conventions. No part of this book may be reproduced in any manner whatsoever without written permission from the publisher, except in the case of brief quotations embodied in critical articles and reviews.

Publisher: Leah Huete de Maines
Editor: Christen Kincaid
Cover Art: Jamie L. Smith
Author Photo: Jamie L. Smith
Cover Design: Elizabeth Maines McCleavy

Order online: www.finishinglinepress.com
also available on amazon.com

Author inquiries and mail orders:
Finishing Line Press
PO Box 1626
Georgetown, Kentucky 40324
USA

Contents

Stingray 1

≈

The Lightyears 3
Flawed Mythologies: I 5
Rat Nest: An Origin Story 6
When We Were Yong I Never Lost or Won 9
In the Closet (with Alice) 10
Hampton Beach 11
Training Ground 12
Flawed Mythologies: II 13
On My Best Days 14
Flooring 15
Flawed Mythologies: III 19

≈

Leap Years 22
Nocturne 23
Flawed Mythologies: IV 25
About Violence 26
In Praise of Variance 27
Lycanthrope 28
When I Listened to the Blasey Ford Hearings 30
Hivemind 31
Flawed Mythologies: V 32

≈

The Flightless Years 34
Perhaps Because I Have Neither 35
Prayer Roulette 36
House Ants 37

The Good Place 39
Mantacore Explains What Went Wrong at the Mirage 40
Forgive Me, Alice 41
Good Housekeeping 42
Lost Highway 44
Flawed Mythologies: VI 46
Glass 47

≈

Near the End of the First Year 51
Flawed Mythologies: VII 52
Summer, 2016 53
West 29th Street Lullaby 55
Outside of Neverland 56
Flawed Mythologies VIII 57
The Great Attractor 58
Last Outing 59
Acceptance 60
What I Thought Was Light Pollution Was Really God 61
To the Dead Man Living Inside My Knee 62
Revisiting Tohono Chul, for Alice, 13 Years Later 64
Flawed Mythologies: IX 65
Bryant Park 66
Enough 67

≈

Notes & Acknowledgements 69

For Jenna Breiter, Mya Green, and Jess Tanck, none of whom are Alice.
≈

In memory of J (1989-2012).
With love for LAH.

≈

Stingray

Show me who you are, not
who you think I want you to be,
she says, and I untie my bathrobe.

That's not what I meant,
she laughs, traces her pinky
down my surgical scar,

circles the birthmark
on my left knee. I tongue away
the stingray

inked to her clavicle. *To die
is different
from what anyone supposed,*

luckier, she reads
from the tattoo
on my right thigh.

Enough words for tonight.

The Lightyears

            When we lived in the Spaceship
our silver-blue trailer

I dreamed of rocketing   across   the Keiper belt
           past Scorpius

towards   the Magellanic Clouds   or at least becoming

Amelia Earhart

disappearing—   That was after
burning beams

crashed to the farmhouse floor   after we got out
         but the cows didn't   before ash-gray
upholstery

and the moonroof   that wouldn't close

           When the heater broke

my mother taught me   a single lit tea candle
is   warmth enough

for a winter night
in a '97 Geo Tracker   Come summer

we camped beneath the stars   on Jupiter's coast
        She told me

about Sputnik's launch
        Apollo's fall   the coverage she'd watched

with a group of kids   in her high school gym
        There was Red Roof

and the Vagabond Inn   After   she pinned
glow-in-the-dark constellations

to my new room's ceiling   The Big Dipper
Libra and Vega

stayed   fixed   there
            until the leak spread

                                    We launched again—

Flawed Mythologies: I

I learned to be right-handed by transcribing pages of Edith Hamilton's *Mythology* with my left hand taped behind my back. I rewrote Sisyphus, again, again, the rock pushed uphill always rolling back.

My mind returns to and recycles the myths, decades since I first touched the worn cover with its red gorgon head held aloft by Perseus. When my friend J died, I thought of them again.

Are the Gods still Gods if they behave in evil ways? I couldn't reconcile who J was to me with the crime I found out he committed.

The myths predate forgiveness. Lighting, fire, wrath, and flood—the early Gods were invested in violence. I don't know when this changed, when we came to believe in supreme benevolence. In the time before forgiveness there was only revenge or rescue.

The *Timeless Tales of Gods and Heroes* are inherently contradictory. There is no rectifying this or making a cohesive account of their lives and relationships. Take Artemis for instance: a midwife goddess responsible for the protection of young girls, she also demanded child sacrifice.

I can see how contradiction splits us into different people. My mother taught me that. Remember, Chronos swallowed his children whole. Time consumes us.

Rat Nest: An Origin Story

I was once a country rat,
napping in the hayloft with my cousins

until our hair glinted cinder-hot,
then dipping our grubby feet

into the creek out back,
sprigs of clover tucked behind our tiny ears.

Weren't we cute
and filthy, frightening the neighbors

as we crept onto their porch steps
to steal blankets and eggs? We were

the jagged teeth
smiling up from storm drains, small bodies

tumbling from the crooks of trees.
You'd hear us scurry and clink

skirting your rafters at dawn. Forgive us
our lice

and the shit we tracked across your kitchens
while you slept. We were often drunk

on moonshine
canned amongst radishes and beets

in our parents' work-sheds,
the bottles of apple-wine wedged

into woodpiles. We ripped
into your ricebags and pocked the lawn

with holes from our treasure hunts:
our buried stashes of cigarettes,

snuff, walnuts, and water-damaged
porno mags

stolen from our uncles' root cellars.
This was years before turnstiles

and grimy tile, before I heard, "Please,
stand clear of the closing doors"

for the first time. Long before
my claws scratched the tracks

that stitch these tunnels together
and the bright bowels of my beloved city

opened, I chewed my way through
the dark clay foundation

eroding beneath the weight
of my family. Our many heads

and naked tails
knotted, writhing into a rodent mass,

we gnawed each other's necks and palms
bloody, clamoring for space

to breathe. We were too many
and not enough

bread. Our parents ate
their soft-boned young

and punched holes through the cabinets
with their teeth. So, gas us. Try

to drive us out with arsenic
or worse

those sticky traps that fastened us
forever there. We'll keep

shredding bedsheets, biting,
and singing our way

through your walls at night.
You should know

we are legion. Light
the damned match—

you can't
kill us all.

When We Were Young I Never Lost or Won

Before aspens burst into green buds and tub suds
dried to brown grime, before the cement

on West 29th street set with pigeon claws
printed in, before our uncles came back from the war,

and lightning-storms crackled all night, back
when our walls were painted lead gray, three or four

of us would lie in the road, backs hot against black asphalt.
The first to get up when a car came

lost. We played the game with trains too, before
a freight engine bore down and erased

the boy who didn't get out of the way—
Sometimes when the subway shakes me awake

I wonder, still, whether resignation,
or will, latched his heels to that track.

In the Closet (with Alice)

Summers passed, we smoked
sour diesel until paint

peeled from the yellowing walls,
legs tangled to fit

our cubic meter of space.
We blew rings against the door

we'd carved our names into.
Vertigo spun us—a tight

knot of limbs nested
in old cotton nightgowns.

When we knew her mother
was coming home

we'd scuttle out, come back
later to collect the roaches.

We hauled ass to her bathroom,
sprayed a haze of perfume

and body mist. Her mom
caught us

showering off the hotbox sweat
one day. For fuck's sake

girls, you're too old for that.
This isn't a locker room.

Her mom must have known
the scent we left

couldn't have come from hair
burnt on her straightening iron.

Hampton Beach

State-colored waves rock
back on themselves, lunge
towards the blustery shore
where my mother is
forever poking
a stingray's wet gills
with a twig. Keep Still!
She'll hiss, as I grip
her frayed flannel sleeve.
This morning the ray
won't thrash back to life
so I don't have to
pull the bloody barb
from her heel as she
screams. Always the wave
breaks over us and
I breathe saltwater
in and out, sinking
down through the silty
deep, until the sea-
floor beneath me shifts,
a reef becoming
the unfinished walls
of our last living
room where I scavenge
under couch cushions,
slip photos from frames,
and unscrew the dead
bulbs from our desk lamps
thumbing the sockets
seeking whatever
switch, riddle, or key
will free me before
gray water gushing
beneath that jammed door
submerges us both.

Training Ground

Spiders large enough to have souls
prowled the ball field, swollen abdomens
banded neon orange, yellow.

That year we fell asleep to Milošević reports.
Uncles and cousins positioned salt and pepper shaker
snipers on Thanksgiving tables—

insurgence and exodus. War meant escape
from rusted cars on brown lawns, knuckles
knotted by factory and farm work.

We tied dishcloths around our faces, drew
a dirt line dividing the playground,
and swung from monkey-bars

showering shaken coke on enemies below.
Recess ended. (The war never did.) Kids
kept finger-guns pointed in hallways, flicked

spitball bullets, stabbed uncoiled paperclips
into desks and hands. Everybody got hit.
It didn't matter if you weren't playing.

Flawed Mythologies: II

I learned to drive by hydroplaning in the hospital parking lot, sitting on a phone book so I could see over the steering wheel of my mother's forest green Geo Tracker. I stood on the gas as she cranked the wheel towards the passenger side, and we did donuts until the security guard came.

Some games were less fun.

My mother believed she was immortal, so she wouldn't fall when she climbed the pines beside the house to swat down wasp nests gathering in the eaves. With every sting she swore and told me fear was undignified.

This was the game: she would say, "Hit me," and I would refuse, and she would pout and say, "Why don't you want to play with me?" I would exhale, and she would say, "Make a fist." She taught me to place my thumb outside my curled fingers so it wouldn't snap on impact. Then she backed me into a corner between the blue settee and the hutch. The skin on my chest went electric, and she screamed, "HIT ME!"

And I did, and I ran. I hid in the closet behind her secret Jim Beam until she went to sleep.

My mother wanted me to be able to defend myself—I was getting picked on in school. At the time I was still transcribing the myths and my favorite movie was the Disney version of Hercules. I wanted to believe my mother was training me to be who I was meant to be.

Because my mother was a God, we went swimming in thunderstorms. The sons and daughters of Poseidon could walk across water without getting wet. My mother believed.

It took me well into adulthood to understand that in her mind there was never any danger. Because she was immortal, lighting would never strike, the car would never flip, my thumb would never break, the men she led me to—my light up sneakers like a lure—would never hurt me. She felt betrayed by my agnostic doubt.

I used to think my mother was Persephone because she would disappear for seasons. When she was gone, I would hunt potato bugs in my grandmother's garden, their yellow shells like beads on the soft green plants.

On My Best Days

I remember you up to your elbows
in potting soil. Hyacinth

bulbs nested in a wooden trough—
how you knew they needed

indirect light, a fall burial.
How the leaves died back.

Plexiglass fortified by wire,
unopenable windows,

shoelaces and belts
surrendered at the check-in desk

are not the artifacts that resurface.
I don't think

of your threadbare open-backed robe
or those soft-soled

slippers you wore
even after your release, shuffling

to the mailbox
on summer afternoons.

I remember you
knew the shoots needed

a good drenching
once the soil dried, how you kept

singing to them
almost every morning

though I think
we both knew

they never would bloom.

Flooring

[Asphalt]

Smashed glass glittered like stars in the headlights of oncoming cars. She, let's call her Alice, pulled off her boots and danced barefoot on Bleecker and Grove, a cascade of rain from the red awning soaking her shoulders.

[Leaves]

Fall blaze. My cousins and I chase each other through a grove of black walnut trees, rolling our ankles on fallen seeds. Dusk still smells like a burnt match head. The cold hasn't yet begun.

[Railroad Ties]

Third grade. We walk the rail bridge over the turtle pond and splash gravel down into the murky water. The first to jump when the train comes loses.

[Hardwood]

I can't remember his face—the boy who didn't jump. After it was rebuilt, re-listed, I went back to my mother's house. Turns out there were hardwood floors all along, underneath the ragged brown carpet. The realtor told me.

[Peanut Shells]

Alice brushed peanut shells off her knee after she rose from proposing to me in a dim bar in Memphis. I crushed my cigarette in the ashtray and kissed her.

[Dovetails]

You can use a jigsaw to shape wood so that it fits together without screws or nails.

I still don't know how they puzzle together: my mother—the boy—Alice.

[White Linoleum]

Fluorescent glare. Disinfectant scent like citrus and old smoke. My mother's metal chair carves four dark arches as she leans forward and back, forward and back, forward…the poster on the wall says, 'Never Give Up.'

[Dirt]

Sun-baked strawberry leaves curled brown—my mother and I bury a coffee can. I put in a toy Dalmatian, his spots rubbed pale, green sea glass, a shiny bit of gravel, a roll of dollar bills. My mother puts in an old photo of us. She slips the money into her back pocket when she thinks I'm not looking.

[Varnished Pine]

I traced knots with the tip of my toe and thought of the boy on the tracks and Alice in the bar and my mom walking across the living room and wondered how I wound up in the suburbs.

[Shag]

If you get anxious, take off your shoes and make little fists with your toes. Shag is the best rug for this.

[Green Linoleum]

My mother's forearm pale against it, almost glowing, bathed in bathroom light. I drop a vile of perfume and it shatters.

[Black Walnut]

The soles of our shoes stuck a bit with each step, and I rubbed up on Alice like a cat romancing a shaft of light.

[Pink Subway Tile]

After the rain-dance she left two muddy footprints on her way to the shower, a few flecks of glitter on the rosy enamel by the drain. For a while I left them and would trace my fingertip over her heel print.

[Grass]

My mother asks if I've ever been on the tracks. I say no. After the boy's funeral I pick wild strawberries from the graves and eat them.

I still dream about him sometimes.

[Gravel]

Ground down beneath car tires—crunch and snap. I jolt awake every time I hear it and hide in the closet behind my mother's piles of books and bottles. After she's gone, I still hear it.

I live miles from gravel now—I still hear it.

[Char]

The black crumbles beneath boot soles the way night-terrors disintegrate once a light is turned on. When I pressed my nose into my mother's flannel, the smoke still clung, months later. The foreman called it a controlled burn.

[Lacquer]

Watching black lacquer seep into wood grain, I'm trying to explain to Alice that I let go of a boy's hand and jumped, and I fled the house before my mother lit the match, so sometimes I struggle to attach.

I loved her though. My mother. Alice. I loved that boy too.

[Rubber Mats]

Du-dum, du-dum, du-dum, du—cowboy boots on rubber mats. Some women sound like light horses when they walk. My mother was one of those women. The mares nickered when her heel hit the ground. Dust glimmered in constellations around the lamp in the haymow, haloing her dark hair.

[Glass]

I remember stepping out on the clear platform, the boy with the lost face holding my hand as we hovered, suspended like a set of quotation marks high above the street. The CN Tower.

When the train came, and his heels wouldn't unplant themselves, what was it he called out to us? I almost remember.

Flawed Mythologies: III

If you traded everything in your life for just one thing, would you give up that one thing to get it all back?

My first all-consuming task was to remind my mother how kind, self-sacrificing, and brilliant she was, how she had helped so many children in her work as an advocate, how she gave up evenings, weekends, and holidays to stay in her office talking with families in crisis—these things were true.

When she brooded and locked herself in her room, my job was to remind her how good she was. I got good at it. It got harder, and one day I met Bacchus in my mother's closet. Drinking wasn't an escape. I drank so I could stay, so that the burning in my chest would go away and I could do my job.

I went to visit my mother in the underworld once. Everyone wore blue gowns and soft slippers, and Hades told me she should stay longer. I wanted her home. I wanted him to keep her.

If I were a hero, would I still remember the porcupine drunk on fermented apples who fell from my mother's tree, or the slow jazz of gin nibbling ice in a glass as the anthem I tuned my youth to? I remember the drowned moth I tried to resurrect, blowing his damp wings back to powder.

Last week on the subway I learned about the value-of-a-statistical-life metric reading Bloomberg Business Review. To reduce risk of fatality, how much would you give?

When I evaluate my life, I can't calculate the cost of clinging to my mother in the lake, her body the buoy when my arms tired. I remember her holding me. I remember her holding me under water until I inhaled silt. Then she saved me. Which fact matters more? She was just playing.

I have a recuring dream where pennies and nickels pour from my purse, a cascade of silver and copper like sloughed fish scales. I sift out loose ibuprofen, gum wrappers and receipt scraps and my mother asks, "Is that all you have?" I unstick every penny from the lips of dried fountains, grip coins in my fists so she won't leave me alone. When I wake, my mouth tastes metallic.

Mythic figures are often conflated. She loved me. She was dangerous.

I didn't leave because I hated her (I did hate her then). I left because the day it occurred to me I could, the sky widened.

I can tell you why Icarus went too high.

Leap Years

On a rooftop in Brooklyn
summer's fetid-garbage scent

settles into our skin
as the sun melts behind

the Domino sugar factory sign,
its dead neon

glowing alive.
The dome of the sky becomes

clear to us—a half-sphere
lit at its edges, a cat's-claw-moon

caught at the apex.
This is how it ends, my friend

laughs, cups his hands, snaps
his palms apart, Pop!

Like those globe terrariums
we had as kids? I ask.

Exactly, we're the ants.

Nocturne

I.

Night-blooming cereus erupts
from my chest, spreads red

onto clean cotton sheets.
Each breath roots me

to the mattress. I never can
move. Who are you? I ask

the man in a dark suit
at the edge of my bed.

That doesn't matter now,
he says.

II.

Apples
thunk to the sidewalk,

split. I smoke clove cigarettes,
forget—

III.

Some dreams
I hold him while he burns,

skin charring into bark
beneath my palms. I hold him

until he's fully cypress,
sap lighting

his fine needles. Please
don't leave me, I think,

but it's his thought
flowering in my head.

Flawed Mythologies: IV

J and I met in boarding school. After room-checks we would go to Café Santé, a restaurant owned by a bon-vivant filmmaker J was dating. Our initials were scrawled across glass tables in cocaine as place-markers.

I'd pull J's red ringlets and he'd chase me behind the bar where we'd pack the espresso machine so tight steam would burst the valve. We'd get kicked out and rush down to the abandoned car we used as a fridge—amber, blue, green, and clear bottles cluttering the trunk.

Artemis must have been jealous watching Orion weave through the tall grass tracking deer. She was too maidenly to be perceived as male, yet too masculine in her pursuits to be considered feminine. A warm envy bloomed in my throat when I watched J dance. He was a ballroom champion. I was strong but not graceful, always feeling a little more boy than girl. I liked girls. J was the first person I told.

Snow collected in my Orion's flame-colored hair, half-moon bruises beneath his blue eyes deepening as he smiled. We made angels on the floor below the broken window of the foreclosed apartment we hung out in. J told me that before his brother died, he had started palming Opana from his bedside table. That's how his drug use began. I kissed a snowflake off his left cheek, and we fell asleep in the cold.

Under the influence of a spell, Orion lunged after a nymph in the forest, but Artemis drew her bow and fired on him before he could strike. She fastened his belt into the dark vault of the sky and sent him into exile. If I'd had that power to cast my friend into the stars, I would have—before the boy I loved grew up and became a man who overpowered someone else and then shot stardust into his own veins.

The news reached me in pieces. I knew J was dead before I learned he had overdosed. Then I was told he was awaiting sentencing for rape.

For months after he died, I looked at the sky and simply said, "Fuck you," which I'm told is still a form of prayer.

About Violence

I couldn't describe his face
but for months after, I saw it on every man

turning a street corner too fast or standing
behind me in line at the supermarket.

In Praise of Variance

Some nights we'd pick fights
over things like which oil best fries
fries or whether it's *all intents or all intense*

and purposes; because a broken vase
is a broken vase, whichever frustration smashes it
against the wall, but sometimes

it's nice to apologize
for something besides being
broke and unable to buy brand-named clothes

or bologna. My mother taught me
there's a certain grace in giving up
on the hope of relief.

Each of the six grayscale petals
of the palm-sized lily tattooed on my left side
was a new sensation—

the skin near my belly split apart
as if being carved, near my back, an incessant
scratching as pigment clawed into skin

like a manic kitten I couldn't shoo away, the ribs
all hot vibration and climb. Sometimes I buy things
just to remind myself

I can. Ink teaches me, again and again,
how even the pains that don't stop
can still change.

Lycanthrope

My sun rises fast,
high before noon, mellow, so no, I don't

want to talk it out—
the wake, flowers I forget to send when

our friends are ill, pills
I don't remind you to take. Our failures

duplicate the way
flames lap gasoline. Those old mushroom caps

you claim drilled blackholes
in your pristine brain—indigo cosmos

exploding inside
you—did I ask you to eat them? Alice,

let's watch Sirius
rise while you sip absinth and I tell you

about the latest
Lazarus taxon revelation: dogs

thought long extinct, found
roaming the bush in Brazil. You'll half-listen,

legs splayed across
our frayed white carpet. Your pearls leave imprints

between my thighs,
a rosary I'll trace home when you go.

You should go, Alice.
We both know my psyche splits—hackles raised

by my fifth gin, meanness
froths up from my lips. Come last call I'll be

snarling at ghosts
you don't see. You should know I'll keep chasing

until I learn how to speak.

When I Listened to the Blasey Ford Hearings

Not the man in my apartment,
or my mom's old boyfriend saying,
it won't happen again, not

my friend who raped a woman, no.
It's the gray room I go back to—

two cops—a woman who says
nothing, and a man in uniform
who says I seem *agitated*.

He's eating Doritos.
He wants clear narrative—linear—words
like *erect* and *flaccid*. Do I remember

a birthmark?—any unusual potentially
defining aspect of the man's anatomy—
       Think hard, he says.

A dull yellow pencil nests
in the slightly open desk drawer.
I describe

billabong flowers
on blue swim-trunks, a ring snagged
in wet hair—

This information
       isn't useful, he says.

Hivemind

After the soldiers spilled out,
all was quiet besides
the dull whir of drones
nesting inside
my skull, humming:

> Maybe we
> were better—

When our rage rises
a red pollen cloud
of coarse-fuzzed bodies
revs their wings
—zing! That first sting
shot up my wrist,
reverb

from a pool stick struck
against a man's ribs.
He hit
that floor.
I left
before

> Maybe—

I swung again
(I would have
called it self-
defense).

> Maybe we
> were better people
> once.
>> Maybe
>> just younger—
>> more forgivable.

Flawed Mythologies: V

When J told his family he was gay, his father told him that the wrong son had died. I wanted to blame some part of J's crimes on his father, on his desperation to prove himself as a man, but I can't. There's no excusing what he did.

Maybe the belief that you're unlovable, or that you've done something unforgivable, underlies most addictions. I felt that sting when I left my mother. Most days I don't anymore.

For the majority of my drinking days, I had blackout-nymphs. I would come to and discover the paper due that afternoon was written, and the laundry had been done. I began as a dull drunk. I burnt out young. Mine wasn't the sort of epic downfall myths are written about. At best I might have come up in *Part Six: The Less Important Myths, or perhaps Brief Myths Arranged Alphabetically.*

But eventually, every bottle became Pandora's box. When Pandora lifted the lid, the residue that stuck to the rim, the one evil that didn't escape, was hope.

As much as I hated the fighting game when I was young, it served me well later in bar fights. Or so I'm told. My mother once clubbed a man to the ground with a metal flashlight on our front porch. Decades later I repeated the same performance with a pool cue when a man cornered me. I am my mother's daughter.

She was like Zeus, rarely hitting me but striking the things around me so they would break—the chair smashed into the kitchen counter, glasses and flatware colliding with the wall.

I am my mother's daughter. J was his father's son. Some violences transmit from generation to generation. But our actions were our own.

The Flightless Years

You're slight enough to slip between the bars
and if you could only refrain from song,

no one would notice you gone. But someone
feeds you, runs a finger over your breast

and says, Hi pretty, in a way that makes
you stay. Maybe you'll nibble her earring

tugging gently until she kisses you,
takes you in her hands and lets you sleep tucked

inside her shirt. Will you dream of rising
high above this city until your house

is lost amongst the patchwork blocks? If you
love her, blue parakeet, then please, teach me

to fan my wings contentedly
                    confined inside this cage.

Perhaps Because I Have Neither

I've never bothered to learn the difference
between Patience & Fortitude.

One, chest proudly puffed, the other tilts
his stoic head as snow settles against his spine

and a man in a blue raincoat climbs him, rides him,
snaps a selfie.

Stone lions preside over pedestrians rushing
sleeted streets, the woman teaching her toddler

to walk those hungry steps—it's all the same to them,
our hustle and hush—they receive us the same.

In a colder city, they might have been defaced
ragged red graffiti blanketing gray manes.

Could they survive where I'm from? My country
is not a country, it's winter, and ice like that snaps

marble, our headstones crumbling.
That hairline crack in Patience would split.

It isn't Fortitude that keeps me here
but fear I've weathered this city too long to endure

anyplace else. I resent the idiot in the blue raincoat
because truth be told

I've always wanted to ride—
lion between my thighs striding down 5th Avenue.

I know they don't love me,
but when I place my hand on their flanks

they give back whatever warmth or cool they have
and what more could I ask for?

Prayer Roulette

Remember the evening I won
fifteen hundred dollars because I stayed

mounted on a mechanical bull? All that cash
blown on Dos Equis and coke. Hit a split

at the blackjack table, doubled-down and won
and won until I blew that too—lost

tokens choked down a slot machine throat
in the Reno airport. Remember that

God, how it used to be—how I thanked you
when I didn't miss my final boarding call

and we celebrated with in-flight champagne?
Nothing within me says stop or slow down,

so you know I'll stay on the velvet blue
bedspread of this woman

who may not really love women, while her body
folds around her gold-haired dog

whose nose is nestled between my knees
and I'll rub their backs while they sleep. God,

you made me this way—I've never prayed
to win, just not to lose,

so maybe
you owe me this one. I'm sorry

I feel closest to you
when you might,

might not,
come through.

House Ants

Somehow
the shower ants
make me happy:

tiny-legged ellipses,
a wavy hair
tracing up pink tile…

They're only there
on summer mornings,
an orderly parade of mouths

carrying crumbs,
bits of dust and skin.
They never blunder or run

into the wall's small crack,
but march steadily towards
that gabardine dark,

their mandibles too loaded
for discourse or argument.
Can I atone

for a childhood spent
gathering them
into terrariums,

separate from their queen,
trapped with the small red spider
I accidentally put in?

What if I dip
a teaspoon into gray water
at the mouth of the drain

and one bedraggled ant
clings to the arched metal
water falling from him until

his antennae raise
and six gold legs
lift his amber body

a fraction of a millimeter?

The Good Place

Adrift in the wide rest-beat between thoughts,
I stand barefoot in the wine cellar, roll
old bottles label-up in their cradles.

I don't group them by rosé/red/white, no.
I'll show you my foiled mosaic: corks pulled
forward into one gold bird in flight/bro-

ken Zen circle/fleur-de-lis/uppercase
A/J. Catacomb workers do this too—
arrange bones into small jokes. I know where

the pinot/Dom/Veuve Clicquot should all go—
I'll rehome the empties by sunset/rise.
I'm at my loneliest when I'm happy.

Mantacore Explains What Went Wrong at the Mirage

Clenching my jaws
around

the sweat-salted flesh
just above

the showman's
rhinestone studded collar

was easy,
as it would be for you

to bite through
an unshelled

soft-boiled egg.
He loved me—

thought love
blunted teeth.

Forgive Me, Alice

You know part of the story—
how the road ended at a gas station
outside Amarillo

where a man in sandy overalls said,
You be careful now,
and I thought,

What the fuck am I doing here?
But my bag was packed before that.
Truth is, a long-tongued dog

lapped at my heels that year,
rabid craving shredding my chest
into hives and I

didn't tell you. I just drove southbound,
outpaced the snow. Before I left,
I meant to teach you

to bleed the radiators—
unscrew steam valves, let heat scream,
water seep, so we could sleep, or you could

sleep without me
groaning over those dripdrip restless nights.

I meant to fix it.

Good Housekeeping

[Pine-Sol]

Pretend the evergreen scent has always penetrated the thick walls of your den. Begin in the corner farthest from the entrance and remember to mop backwards so you erase your shoeprints as you go.

[Dawn]

Go before dawn. After you've washed every plate and packed them all in cloth-sided boxes topped with shredded documents or crumpled newspaper. Don't forget the bowls gathering dust on top of the cabinets, the red-willow China you've never used and haven't yet smashed.

There are boxes you will never unpack.

[Windex]

Streak-free. Swallows broke their necks weekly, until my mother crashed through the plate glass door.

[Shop-Vac]

Sucks up everything from damp plaster to glass, every lost earring back and nail-clipping.

[Ajax]

Mildly abrasive, best of the scouring powders for the soap scum and limescale ringing your tub. When my mother went away, I learned to take care of things. Scrub away the rust/grime/blood. Use gloves. Repeat as many times as needed.

[Mr. Clean]

There is no Magic Eraser.

Before I've left each house, apartment, and hotel room I've lived in, I've etched something into the doorframe's edge or the underside of a closet shelf.

[Hefty Bags]

If sliced apart and bordered with duct tape, a black jumbo trash bag can successfully cover a door-sized hole. Choose which side you want to be on before you finish.

[Tide]

What unsettles more, retreat or return? High, low, high. Repeat as needed. Laundry is never truly done, unless you do it naked. High.

Empty the lint trap. Low. Check for any lost socks or dollars.

[Colgate]

When you run out of spackle from filling in the major scars, mask all remaining nail-holes with white toothpaste. Rub away the excess with your shirt sleeve after it dries.

No one will notice until after you've gotten your security deposit back.

[Pledge]

You still won't get your deposit back. Leave no forwarding address.

Lost Highway

I.

On the outskirts of Meteor Crater
my small blue SUV glides
into moon-glare. Tonight

the world's largest ball of twine
unraveled, and I followed
this black highway

shot through
with cautionary yellow stitching
that knits Kansas

to the red sands past Albuquerque,
past those Flagstaff roadrunners
rushing dust trails

like earthbound comets.

II.

Pinprick flashes in darkness—
no tail or headlights,
not for hours.

One night, years ago,
I wandered, unaware as cloud,
weightless—whatever

I there was
diaphanous as ash
flicked

from the passenger side
window.

III.

Is this the road, or have I
unspun again? The desert's end,
flat and black as space, the earth

bottomless as the well
we dropped quarters in
as children, waiting

small forevers
to hear that clink, or the well
we all fall in

on the brink of sleep, jerking
back, jaws snapping like carp
alarming our bedmates.

V.

The moon comes
close enough to kiss the road
with her full face, the way

Alice surfaced through
the bright cistern I'd
dissolved into, slapped

and slapped my face,
calling me
back into my body

and wherever I was
released.

Flawed Mythologies: VI

To pursue Artemis is to pursue ruin. She leaves a wake of dead huntsmen as her story progresses. I was never what my heroes were chasing.

Opiates flood your system with oxytocin—the neurochemical equivalent of love. I'm lucky that felt dangerous to me.

Years ago, a batch of heroin called Raptor led to a dozen overdose deaths in New York and New Jersey. It was cut with Ajax. Before Raptor there was Icarus. The tiny bag had a red wing stamped on its side.

Once, Alice and I rode horses and talked about reincarnation. She wanted to return as a flower in May. I wanted wings, sparrow maybe, something sky-bound.

Two days before her first overdose, I asked Alice if she remembered riding real horses—so much warm muscle and hair flying, hooves beating beneath us. She nodded, but she wasn't answering me.

I couldn't blame her. I remember the warm field. The way we rode into stratosphere, while our bodies stayed in somebody's basement or on the bathroom floor of a fast-food restaurant—that's where they found one of our friends that summer.

Icarus and Raptor taught us that the glue tethering you to yourself can melt. J, Billy, Anthony, David S., David C. R., Edwin, Kevin, Alice, Casey, Greg, James, Alice, Vicky, Alice…

In drug-speak, when someone injects for the first time, they say they've *gotten their wings*. This is the story of Pegasus, the white horse the heroes rode to freedom.

Glass

[Stained]

As in church windows or red wine residue.

[Broken]

As in car window or "wear thick-soled shoes."

[Devlin]

Typically formed into a small latched-box: rosé, violet, or sky-blue hue. Nothing in that box is sacred, but it appears more precious than it really is. Alice kept hair pins inside that looked like the tusks of miniature mammoths.

[The Imperial Glass]

The most expensive (empty) Champagne glass in the world is valued at $85,365 per unit. I would break it immediately.

[Shatter-proof]

Back to car windows, which break like ice (crushed or cubed) rather than jagged like a wine glass or storm-window.

[Mirrored]

Seven sycamore trees line Fulton Street outside St. Paul's Trinity Church, reflected by thousands of bank, hotel, and apartment windows: The Financial District Forest, Manhattan.

[Retail Window]

Some storefronts distort your form into a lovable reflection. In others, the effect is freak-show. The point is always that the jeans are beautiful, and you can see yourself in them though they are currently apart from you. It's a kind of Eros established by high-resolution plexiglass tinted to make the viewer appear tan and slender.

[Bullet-Proof]

Bushwick bodega. It yellows like nicotine over time, amber darkening with exposure. The encasement on Knickerbocker was so scratched I never got the full effect of the clerk's face in the years we went every day for ice cream and cigarettes.

[Lead Crystal]

High refraction index. Shatters on impact. Counter to borosilicate glass which is heat resistant.

[Chihuly]

"…the way form interacts with light and space…installations are created in dialogue with the environments in which they are sited, interacting harmoniously while affecting spatial relations to inspire profound experiences…" Gorgeous. Frequently looks like sperm.

> See: Kew Gardens, London.
> See: Bronx Botanical Garden circa 2016.
> See the sculpture in the hotel lobby, where we said hello and goodbye for the last last time.

[Fused Quartz]

The sidewalk concrete within a three-block radius of Grand Central is mixed with chemically pure silica so the paths cast a shimmer beneath the halogen streetlights. Combined with the scant layer of smashed soda-lime and headlight fragments on the surface, the effect is double-glitter, stars beneath your feet as you walk.

Near the End of the First Year

Swaying slightly from a powerline
a pair of black high-tops

casts a shadow on the asphalt,
mottling the double-yellow-line.

Why this is the evening
I notice them

and looking west, catch the light
dyeing the Hudson rose,

I don't really know. Why tonight
the electrical simmer

skirting my inner world
                    cuts off—

and all at once,
though they've been nattering

all summer—
                cicadas.

Flawed Mythologies: VII

The gate leading out of the underworld is said to be guarded by a three-headed dog. I never met Cerberus. The moment I got sober, in retrospect, came when I was sitting on the curb outside an Arby's in my ripped jeans, my friend's ten-year-old daughter braiding my hair while her mom fished her lost cell phone from beneath the deli counter.

Who knew that would be the moment?

Hands shaking lightly, my pulse a drunk stagger climbing subway steps. The girl loved me. And I didn't know why. At that moment something unlocked, a long-stuck gate-latch slid back in my psyche—this world visible though not yet entered.

If my mother had been anyone different, would I still love the people who've meant the most to me? I wouldn't trade my chosen family for a better mother, for unbreaking my thumb or relocating my shoulder, or learning to swim in a pool instead of a lightning-bright lake. Maybe that's never been the equation, but it's the formula that gives me the most peace.

Apart from her name and her dominion over the air, little is written about Selene, the third aspect of Artemis. She's a big question mark, just as my mother is after seventeen years apart.

Reconcile—from the Latin *reconciliare*. The prefix *re-* meaning *back* is also an expression of *intensive force,* and *conciliare* breaks down as *to bring together.*

I don't want to unite by force. I refer to my mother in the past tense as a way of creating space in my mind, so I can meet her as the person she has become if we do see each other again.

Summer, 2016

V.

In my throat
a crowd of crows

takes wing
and after

the fifth funeral
I laugh—

it's the only way
to breathe.

Car windows rattle
death-metal reverb,

seat vibrating spine,
scream—

IV.

I don't answer my phone anymore.

III.

Liver disease, we say,
or heart issue.

It's true
until someone asks,

      relapse?

II.

After the second burial
I kiss my friend on the neck,

ask him
to please outlive me.

I.

When he died
I felt too full for sound.

No radio or TV.
Only my cats' feet

on the floorboards,
the moans of doors

opening, closing.
Paper grocery bags

crinkle, an orange
thuds to the floor, rolls

under the stove.
I swear at the orange

as though it's the one
to blame.

West 29th Street Lullaby

The music of the world doesn't change—
car horns arrange, rearrange and blare.

Horns arranged, rearranged and blared,
sirens bouncing red and blue like hummingbirds.

Red and blue hummingbirds bounce—sirens
echoing up the narrow alley throat.

Echoing up the narrow alley throat
like laughter, the metal crash of dumpster trash.

Trash thrown into dumpsters, metal, cash—
7th Avenue searches us for scraps.

7th Avenue searches us for scraps,
unless you live here, you don't know that.

Unless you've lived here, you don't know
how the music of this world
                              doesn't change.

Outside of Neverland

Somehow, every time he got lost in Boston
my friend would find himself

across from Perkins Institute for the Blind.
Maybe that's the way

God works. Like the bat that flapped into my chest
below those vaulted Grand Central stars—

a brown-winged-flurry flickering to my neck,
then gone—and with it

my panic at missing the train, so I texted
an overdue amends to that same friend

who would hold my hand
for the next three years of shopping, karaoke nights,

and funerals. Blessèd are the lost
commuters, for they shall be led to the blind.

Blessèd are the hurried, for they shall be
sideswiped by wings.

Little bat, my sightless savior,
come back. I'm over plotting my own course,

mending the hems of my black dresses, over
pale lilies mixed with baby's breath.

Lord, let the last of my lost boys
age. I'm done

with kneeling, done with waiting rooms,
done with song.

Flawed Mythologies: VIII

In the years since J died, I've come upon scraps of forgiveness like loose change in the street. When Acteon's dogs scattered him across the forest, I wonder if the women searching for pieces of him understood they would never remember him completely.

The last time I watched J dance we agreed we wouldn't drink or get high together anymore. I never saw him again.

I think about the movies we snuck into and how after we saw Troy he ran shirtless around the rugby field reenacting battles with an invisible sword until the stadium lights went out and we collapsed laughing in the grass.

When he was cast as the villain in our school play, I was shocked at his heavy footfalls across the black floorboards, his icy eyes. If the Fates dictated that he had to die, why not cut that cord before he hurt someone?

He was the first boy I let curl around me while we slept. He was the boy who held my hand and told me I should get out of the car the last time I saw my mother.

What metamorphoses could my friend have undergone—or was he the Trojan horse all along, soldiers in his belly waiting to break free?

The night our schoolmate died, J draped his coat over my shoulders and stood in the snow by the river wearing only a t-shirt. I couldn't cry until I pressed my ear against his chest. Would someone evil give up their jacket on a below-zero night?

The Great Attractor

Astronomers first noticed in 1973
that our universe is not

expanding ever-outward
but sinking

southward towards some massive
unknown, hidden lightyears

behind the Zone of Avoidance.
On Crosby Street

I chain-smoke and notice
how snow squalls

seem to dim and flicker
the high-rises' lights, not unlike

the hydrogen star-web
at the crumbling border of Laniakea—

our galaxy filament
being slowly pulled and consumed

by whatever black hole
or unfathomable mass

brings us crashing towards
our neighboring superclusters.

What anomaly governs
our course? How is it my friend

collides with me tonight,
on this icy street

in a city we
no longer live in

       and knocks me off my feet?

Last Outing

J raises his arms into the night breeze
that ruffles his fiery nest of sideburns
like a whisper, unzips his blue fleece, turns
a full circle with his wings unfurled. Leave
me here, he tells me, on top of this grate,
so I can feel the trains grumbling beneath
the street. He shuts his pale eyes and breathes,
rocking back on his boot heels. We're *so* late,
I tell him, we'll miss the train to Greenwich.
Just then the rumble and rush of hot air—
the F train below billows his hair
into a halo. It doesn't matter which
train we get, he says, We had *this*. Promise
you'll do this after I'm gone. I promise.

Acceptance

Each morning before the dogs bark themselves
awake, while haze shrouds driveways and grass blades,

before I make up my face for the day
there's a moment—before knowing knocks

against my skull, like a neighbor angry
my overgrown sunflowers are blocking

the sidewalk. Not a moment, maybe
some pocket unstitched in space, lined with white

static, where the ambulance never came
because I never had to call, and rain

catches porch lights as it falls—a miniscule
meteor shower. And on all those swift

stars shot to grass and asphalt—there's nothing
to bargain—because the worst hasn't been.

What I Thought Was Light Pollution Was Really God

Rosy omni-glow swatches my walls
turning dust into tiny star-drifts. Most nights

I walk beneath constellations of streetlights.
Broadway billboards shuffling neon

ignite that silica shimmer I love—sidewalks
set to glimmer and deflect rain.

Red rolling over blue folded into siren scream—
ambulances I called for my Alices.

Don't think of them. The way it ended. We began
in the grass, on our backs, legs

lifted so we could grind clouds and supernovas
beneath our heels. Imagine the dust

spilling from all those nebulae we might have crushed.
Maybe the old Gods were just

as reckless. Wrong to turn warriors
into zodiacs and birds—

to give them flight—to give them their own
gravity and light.

To the Dead Man Living Inside My Knee

A careless dictator, most days
I do not think of you

unless you protest, beating your fists
against the walls of my flesh

when I've danced you too hard
or damp February

clenches your teeth
into a knot of hot fury. Please

forgive my tendency
to fall up subway station stairs.

This can't be
the afterlife you imagined:

those wobbly cobblestones
skirting Jane Street

we ran in stilettoes
outpacing a chestnut police horse

weaving gridlocked traffic.
Thank you

for not giving up on me.
For kneeling quietly in pew after pew.

What have I given you
but four more presidencies,

hitchhiking three countries,
and countless times

we've fallen asleep
folded over

in economy class? I never
thanked you

for our last dance with Alice,
how you let me lift her

from the conference room carpet
and we kissed California

goodbye. Thank you
for keeping me upright

when the phone sounded
and I knew

before answering—
       I never thanked you

for the way you buckled
but held fast, for the way

we walked on
and on until you screamed

and I hurt less
or differently. Please

keep carrying me.

Revisiting Tohono Chul, for Alice, 13 Years Later

Rabbits still run the courtyard wild
and cacti spears fence the park perimeter
with palm-sized purple blooms
crowning their heads.

A hummingbird tongues pollen from seeds,
emerald cheek gold-dusted as he lifts
above the square—an apostrophe
hung above garden paths

empty of people now, dusk clouds
edging in. Whatever possessed us to dance
in that desert downpour all those years ago?
Alice, the girl I craved like saguaros crave rain,

you raised me into the breeze and we fell
shrieking into mud. What is memory
if not the rain-drenched mud-slathered you
existing within me? Your wet form

folded into my labyrinth so I feel your grit
tangled hair and cold sand studding
your soaked shirt. Standing below
this low-slung sky, I can almost forget

what happens next. Violet-mouthed
flowers pray down the first drop
centimeters from my eye,
a translucent globe splashed open

on red stairs, where tomorrow
a girl in a pink dress might descend, new
patent leather shoes squeaking slightly
with each step—

another entry into the bright kaleidoscope
without you.

Flawed Mythologies: IX

When Persephone returned from the underworld, she rubbed her eyes, shocked by the brightly colored world.

I turn back to the myths when I'm looking for meaning. Although *Mythology* promises to be of no help, somehow that return, that surrender, brings a kind of peace. I love the *Timeless Tales of Gods and Heroes*. I love them even though my shoulder popped out of socket once when I was transcribing them, and my mother adjusted the tape holding my left hand back.

It's the oldest book I know, and though there is no reconciling the contradictions within the characters themselves, or inherent in their relationships with one another, I return again and again.

The question remains—are the Gods still Gods if they behave in evil ways?

I don't know. I know I worshiped my mother at one time, and J was a legend in my mind. I know the different damage each of us has done.

Maybe part of what draws me back is the fact that the Gods were revered and remembered despite their actions. Lavish temples were erected, sacrifices made, and maybe honoring them like that wasn't merely plea for mercy, but proof the Gods were loved, however flawed they were.

Bryant Park

Often, when I'm going to the library,
I don't go inside. I eat

my double-quarter-pounder with cheese
a few seats over

from the Fashion Week spectators, or look
into those gilded Park Terrace windows,

feed sparrows croissant crumbs, or count
tourists emerging from the bellies

of double-decker buses. When pear and cherry
blossoms let go, something like snow

falls and coats the sidewalks,
invades my hair, and I'm in love

with how little I matter
amongst all of it, how the trains below

enter and exit with a sigh. Mostly I've come
to catch my breath

on the granite steps. My friend came once
and scattered ashes on the grass

below a magnolia, returned to find
a picnicking family perched

on that exact spot where what was left
dusted the earth.

Whatever the me of me is,
one day, that too will diffuse, and what's left

will be blown beneath somebody's shoes,
or into the mouths of tulips

the children uncrown in fistfuls.

Enough

A woman's spine arcs into a question mark, back bending to meet
the beat of the street player's sax

on the corner of 42nd & Lex, as a man with ankle-length dreads
strokes the black nose of a carriage horse

idling next to a falafel cart, and a sequined gold miniskirt
negotiates fare, flipping her hair and rocking

back on her spiked heels, pale hands gesturing towards
the hansom-cab driver in his top hat and rosy polo.

The sidewalk catches light, glitters, the skirt catches light, glitters,
cabs honk their song. These nights I want nothing

but to be a thoughtless, walking eye
smiling at the brown Doberman with his crooked underbite.

Notes & Acknowledgements

Deep thanks to the Finishing Line Press team, especially my editor, Christen Kincaid. Thank you for making this book a reality.

My gratitude to the following journals and anthologies in which earlier versions of some poems first appeared:

> *Red Wheelbarrow* (February 2024): Bryant Park
> *New Note Poetry Journal* (October 2023): The Lightyears
> *Fauxmoir* (September 2023): Glass
> *The Write Launch* (September 2023): To the Dead Man Living Inside My Knee and What I Thought Was Light Pollution Was Really God
> *Southern Humanities Review* (Prize Edition, December 2022): Training Ground
> *Allegory Ridge's "Aurora"* (Vol. 2 2021): Enough
> *Tusculum Review*: "Flawed Mythologies" as "Mythology Lessons" (2020)
> *Pigeon Pages* (August 2020): Perhaps Because I Have Neither
> *Peculiar: A Queer Literary Journal* (Issue 8, 2020): Flooring as Flooring Pecha Kucha
> *Indie Blu(e)'s "Smitten: This is What Love Looks Like, Poetry for Women by Women"* (2019): Revisiting Tohono Chul, For Alice, 13 Years Later and In the Closet (with Alice)

An artist's book variation of *Flooring* entitled *Home* was on exhibit in the University of Utah, Book Arts Program's *Booking a Brouhaha* from December 2021-March 2022.

Glass contains a quotation from Chihuly's official site: https://www.chihuly.com/works/installations

The line "my country is not a country, it's winter" in *Perhaps Because I Have Neither* is a translation from Gilles Vigneult's Quebecois folksong, *Mon Pays* (1965).

An earlier version of the *Flawed Mythologies* series was selected by judge David Lazar for *Tusculum Review*'s 2020 Nonfiction Prize and released as a limited-edition chapbook under the title *Mythology Lessons*. This essay was listed as 'Notable' in Best American Essays, 2021.

The essay and this book owe a dept of gratitude to Edith Hamilton's *Mythology: The Timeless Tales of Gods and Heroes*.

The essay was born from Catherine Barnett's prompt: write a lyric essay about a text or work of art you have a relationship with—and I had no idea how far it would go.

Section VII is for Marie and Grace Inan Howe. Thank you for being my gate.

Big thanks and love to the U of U crew(s), especially those who've spent time with this work, and those who've brought such joy to our journey through the Mountain West: Hannah Allen, Allison Field Bell, Audrey Bauman, Stephanie Choi, Diana Clarke, Matty Layne Glasgow, Chengru "Lulu" He (for everything), Emad Jabini, Aristotle Johns, Jasmine Kaliq, Jesse Kohn, Michelle Macfarlane, Corley Miller, Sam Nelson, Erin O'Launaigh, Nick Pierce, Amy Sailer, Samyak Shertok, Max Schleicher, Jess Tanck, Sam Thilen, Lindsey Webb, and Jake Yordy.

Thank you to my mentors there: Scott Black, Katharine Coles, Anne Jamison, Jacqueline Osherow, Marnie Powers-Torrey, and Paisley Rekdal. I've learned so much from you.

This collection was made possible in large part through the support of the Thomas S. Hunter fellowship at CUNY Hunter (2018-2020). My love always to Malibu: Jenna Breiter, Jiordan Castle, Eric Janken, Mari Pack, Sam Reichman, and Vanessa Ogle, for your generous readings and friendship. See you at the diner soon.

With profound appreciation to my mentors there: Catherine Barnett, Lynne Greenberg, Donna Masini, and Tom Sleigh—despite what you say, this would not have happened without you.

For your love and support in various forms across many years: Tina Chang, Martha Rhodes, and Susan Martin Taylor, thank you!

Jamie L. Smith is the author of the chapbook *Mythology Lessons,* winner of Tusculum Review's 2020 nonfiction prize, selected by judge David Lazar. She holds an MFA from Hunter College, where she was the recipient of the Louise DeSalvo Memorial Memoir Prize, the Collie Hoffman Memorial Poetry Prize, the Randolph & Eliza Guggenheimer Prize, the Miriam Wienberg Richter Award, and the Catalina Páez & Seamus MacManus Award sponsored by the Academy of American Poets. She is a Graduate Research Fellow at the University of Utah, where she has been awarded the Levis Poetry Prize, judged by Diana Khoi Nguyen, and the Scowcroft Prose Prize, selected by David Shields. Her work appears in publications including *Bellevue Literary Review, Best New Poets, Not-Very-Quiet, Red Noise Collective, San Antonio Review, Southern Humanities Review, Tusculum Review, The Write Launch, Ruminate, Red Wheelbarrow,* and anthologies by Beyond Queer Words, Indie Blu(e), and Allegory Ridge.

www.ingramcontent.com/pod-product-compliance
Lightning Source LLC
Chambersburg PA
CBHW020341170426
43200CB00006B/451